© 2002 by Barbour Publishing, Inc.

ISBN 1-58660-446-5

Cover art © Eyewire

Published by Barbour Books, an imprint of Barbour Publishing, Inc., P.O. Box 719, Uhrichsville, Ohio 44683, www.barbourbooks.com

Member of the
Evangelical Christian
Publishers Association

Printed in China
5 4 3 2 1

Silent NIGHT

Ellyn Sanna

Silent night, holy night,
All is calm, all is bright,
Round yon virgin, mother and Child,
Holy Infant, so tender and mild.
Sleep in heavenly peace
Sleep in heavenly peace.

CONTENTS

    I. All Is Bright 7

   II. Holy Infant 19

 III. Heavenly Peace 33

At Christmastime,
and all year round,
may your life be lit
by the Christ Child's love,
and may you know His enduring peace.

I

All Is Bright

LIGHT OUT OF DARKNESS

In 1818, in the town of Oberndorf, Austria, on a cold Christmas Eve, the organist discovered the organ could not be used for the evening services. Mice had eaten the leather bellows and ruined it. It seemed there would be no music at Oberndorf's Christmas Eve service.

But Vicar Joseph Mohr and Franz Gruber put their heads and talents together. . .and wrote a new song, one that didn't need the organ but that could be played on a guitar. *"Stille Nacht"* was introduced that night at midnight mass—and today "Silent Night" is sung around the world in more than ninety languages. What appeared to be a tragedy birthed something new and lasting.

As you look at your own life, what births do you see waiting to emerge from the difficulties you may encounter this Christmas season? Human disasters are often the very circumstances that God uses to shine His light into our lives.

VIOLE RUELKE GOMMER

In the beginning the Word already existed.
He was with God, and he was God. . . .
Life itself was in him, and this life gives light to everyone.
The light shines through the darkness,
and the darkness can never extinguish it.

JOHN 1:1, 4

THE LIGHT OF CHRISTMAS TREASURE

Treasure hunting on Christmas morning? Yes, that was our tradition when our children were young. I have no Christmas memories from when I was a child, so I wanted to make Jesus' birthday special for my own family. After sledding, building snowmen, and getting the perfect tree, the treasure hunt for gifts was the highlight of our Christmas celebration. Mysterious envelopes would appear throughout the house, containing directions to each person's special gift.

One year, the directions led our son from room to room and finally to the barn. There he discovered a floppy-eared hound dog waiting in the hay. I can still remember the look on his face when he turned toward his father and me.

"I can't believe he's mine," he whispered with wonder in his voice.

Another year, our daughter even found clues in the woodpile. The last one directed her to the freezer—but the door was shut tight, and she couldn't lift the lid. Luckily, the phone next to the freezer rang just then. It was her grandmother, calling to wish everyone a Merry Christmas. . .and she happened to know where the freezer key was hidden. Our daughter's gift was frozen solid—but she loved the hot pink snowsuit.

Our family will never forget those Christmas treasure hunts. These days, all year long, we still hunt for an even greater treasure. . .the Christ Child, the shining gift that lies hidden in the midst of our lives, always waiting for us to discover Him if we will only look.

BARBARA WYMBS

Light window candles.
Christmas is near.

Strum love guitars.
Christmas is dear.

Celebrate Christ's birth.
Christmas is here.

FLORENCE M. HUSTEDT

THE LIGHT SHED BY SHARING

Our first Christmas as a blended family, Bob and I each brought a thirteen-year-old son to our marriage. We wanted to make this holiday special, something to set the tone for all the shared holidays to come. We both agreed that we should start our life as a family with an emphasis on the real meaning of Christmas. We longed for something that was more than a time to spend money. We hoped to celebrate the true meaning of Christmas by sharing our joy and faith with others.

I don't know who first suggested it, but gradually, an idea took shape in our minds: We would sing our favorite Christmas carol to our landlords, German immigrants in their eighties. We all agreed that if we learned the song in their native language, it would be a wonderful gift from us to them.

So we divvied up the preparation tasks and got started. Bob found an instrumental version of "Silent Night" and recorded it in an endless loop. His son, Bobby, asked his German teacher for the words to the song. My son, Brian, made copies for us—each with phonetic pronunciations. My job was to bake traditional German cookies to offer our landlords along with our song.

Christmas Eve was blustery and bitter, much like the night when our carol was composed. We crept down the stairs to the dark hallway outside our landlords' door.

"Quick, Bobby, plug in the recorder. Brian, ring the bell," Bob whispered.

"Who's there?" our landlord's voice grumbled from behind the door.

The door swung open, and our voices joined in song, just as we had planned, singing the true Christmas carol, rather than the one played by cash registers. *Stille nacht! Heil'ge nacht!* As our confidence grew, so did our volume.

A slow smile softened the face of our crusty landlord. "Frieda! Frieda! Come quick. They're singing to us."

We finished the verse—the only verse we had learned in German—and then they took over and serenaded us with the other verses. We all sang it together in English, and then again in German, their strong voices carrying our halting German in a triumphant swell of song. The joy and warmth on our landlords' faces returned our gift to us a thousandfold. That cold, dark hallway held enough candlepower to outshine the lights of the busiest shopping mall.

Whenever our boys reminisce about the past, they still recall that special first Christmas Eve together. . .a bright, shining moment when we were all lit by the love shed by that Wondrous Child.

MARY LOU KOESTER

You are a kingdom of priests,
God's holy nation, his very own possession.
This is so you can show others the goodness of God,
for he called you out of the darkness
into his wonderful light.

1 PETER 2:9

JOY LIGHT

Beyond my wildest dreams, where my mind cannot grasp or fully comprehend, an announcement is made: good tidings of great joy.

Angels rejoice. Their light illumines cowering shepherds as they praise the heavenly Father. "Glory to God!" they proclaim. The Savior has come to earth. The Son has left His celestial throne. Jesus has entered our world as a helpless baby.

He gave up streets of gold to spend thirty-three years walking the dusty roads of Palestine. He left the angels' honor and praise. . .and received only rejection and blasphemy from those He had created in His own image. In the end, He submitted to a cruel death. Did the angels weep?

After that death, they proclaimed a new announcement: "He is not here." He has risen from the dead, victorious over this world's sin. The angels once more worship at His throne. Will humans still resist His light?

The heavenly host await their orders to announce His return journey to our earth. Because He will come again, our world is full of promise. . .and hope. The joy of those ancient good tidings still shines, even in our darkest hours.

DENISE OAKLEY

*The city has no need of sun or moon,
for the glory of God illuminates the city,
and the Lamb is its light.*

REVELATION 21:23

II

Holy Infant

Miracle Baby

Just for a moment. . .
did stars cease their twinkling?
did clouds hesitate in their course?
did every living creature in the water,
on the land, and in the air become immobile?
did the winds cease?
did mortals pause?
Just for a moment
did absolute silence engulf the earth
as a baby cried?

OR, just for a moment, did
stars twinkle a little brighter;
breezes gust a little faster;
the oceans surge, waves leaping higher,
tossing frothy sprays toward the heavens;
all the rivers of the earth erupt in joyous turmoil;
cold northern lakes regions sing as ice broke,
echoing melodious tones from shore to shore?
Just for a moment,
did all creation rejoice
as a baby cried?

Shepherds raced down a hill.
Heavenly hosts sang "Hallelujah!"
Time divided into two: before and after.
And then, as now, ordinary people went their ordinary way,
Oblivious to the miracle.

MARTHA O. GIRTON

LESSONS OF THE MANGER

"No, mustn't touch," I insisted as I removed the sheep from my granddaughter Malea's small hand. She had a hard time resisting the Christmas decorations I had carefully placed around the living room, and she was especially drawn to the crèche.

I returned the lamb to the fold and attempted to explain in words an eighteen-month-old child could grasp. "See Baby Jesus." I pointed to the manger child.

"Baby," she echoed—a word she knew well. She loved babies, little people like herself.

"Pretty," I said. "But we just look at Baby Jesus. We don't touch."

She seemed to accept my adult babble and turned away after awhile to play with her toys. A moment later, however, she plopped her baby doll right in the middle of the holy scene.

The impact of Malea's baby sent two of the smaller angels flying into all three wise men, who landed facedown at the foot of the manger. The whole flock of sheep skittered across the table, while Joseph wobbled but remained upright beside Mary.

A day or two later, the symbolism of that moment sank into my mind: A Baby had struck our earthly scene, as well—and that heavenly impact brought men of earthly wisdom prostrate before God's Son. The flock spread out into the world. Earthly fathers wavered, but they continued to hang on.

My hands-off-the-Christ-Child attitude changed. After all, Malea had simply brought her baby to the manger to be with the holy Baby. And God comes to us in terms everyone can grasp, in a form that draws all people—even little people like Malea.

GLENDA EMIGH

THE BEST PRESENT

Our family still remembers their favorite Christmas present. My husband and I hid the gift under a big TV box we had rescued from the cellar. The children took turns guessing what could possibly be inside.

"It's a lizard," my son Chip offered.

"How about a parrot?" Sherri asked.

"It's a giant rat," ten-year-old Kelly announced with a giggle.

Finally, my husband said, "On the count of three, I want you to lift the box, okay?"

They nodded and held their breaths in anticipation.

"One. . .two. . .three!" They raised the cardboard container in triumph.

Gasps of surprise were followed by cries of joy and delight as our daughter Pam, a missionary to Guatemala, rose from her crouched position under the box. She had surprised her younger siblings with a Christmas visit—and her presence surpassed any other gift we received that year.

The fond memory of that Christmas reminds me of the Gift we have all been offered, at Christmas and all through the year. He arrived swaddled in plain wrappings. . .yet His coming changed the world forever.

His name is Jesus. . .the best gift God ever gave humanity.

CINDY NOONAN

Jesus Christ brought forgiveness to many
through God's bountiful gift. . . .
We have the free gift of
being accepted by God. . . .
All who receive
God's wonderful, gracious gift of righteousness
will live in triumph over sin and death.

ROMANS 5:15–17

Christmas Party

Cute Santas and cuter snowmen scream the song
from their painted mouths.
James Stewart, Tim Allen, Ed Wynn do their best,
and Sinatra, Bing, and Louis Armstrong croon or belt it out,
while it's explained by Charlie Brown,
singing vegetables, and the green-faced Grinch.

At church, children in bathrobes and aluminum foil crowns. . .
a special adult choir for weeks has gulped down dinner,
then rushed off for practice.
Services with candlelight dripping hot wax on fingers,
a circuit of parties,
covered-dish, like church people everywhere.

Exhausted, we finally stop.
Is this din drowning out a Baby's cries from a stable out back?
Or are we, like the mother of the bride after the big day,
tired from a job well done?

And this party
is only a drop in the bucket
compared to the party we will have
when we see our
Beloved,
risen
shining,
and face-to-face.

LESLEE CLAPP

Birth Pains

Do we really think Emmanuel
   slid
      silently
         into our world
            on a quiet, peaceful night?

My firstborn came
   crying
      kicking
         gasping for air
            as I shivered and shook,
            exhausted from
            panting
              pushing
                praying.

Was Christ's coming less labored?
Or do we sterilize the stable
sentimentalize the saga and
ceremonialize the incarnation
to minimize the birth pains
mother
Son, and
Father
suffered as. . .

God stripped Himself of glory that night,
giving
grieving
groaning
to be one with us
so we could be
one with Him?

PATRICIA SOUDER

MOTHER AND CHILD

I felt twinges and tightenings throughout the day, but I kept on baking and cleaning for a Christmas Eve get-together at our little home. *No point in postponing life for a baby who's already a week late,* I reasoned. Aunts, uncles, cousins, and parents were all invited for a last party BB (Before Baby). At supper, my husband asked, a little nervously, if it was time to go to the hospital.

I shook my head firmly. "I still have a lot to do." As the former head nurse at the hospital's coronary care unit, I was determined not to entertain my colleagues by showing up in false labor.

I continued getting ready for the party. . .but by 11:00 that night, I gave in. "I think it's the real thing," I told Larry. "You might as well take me to the hospital so you can get some sleep"—which, in the early 1970s, was what husbands did while their wives delivered babies.

I, on the other hand, was ushered through heavy metal doors to the Sacred Refrigerator Room designated for labor and delivery in the days prior to birthing suites. Six hours later, shaking and shivering with exhaustion and exhilaration, I called Larry to tell him we had a son. A Christmas Eve son.

I'd missed my own party and would spend Christmas in the hospital. And my son would celebrate all his birthdays in the shadow of the holidays. My prayers to the contrary had been divinely dismissed. I could almost hear God chuckle. Nothing had happened the way I had planned. Yet, as I rested quietly in the maternity ward, I experienced Christmas in a fresh, new way.

Mary and I had already become close friends on the pilgrimage of pregnancy. When I first felt the flutters of life, I reflected on how Mary must have felt, knowing she was carrying God's Son. When I grew enormous with child, I gained a new appreciation for the eighty-mile walk she made right before giving birth. Now, when I thought of going into labor without a room in the inn or a midwife, I suspected she must have wondered why God hadn't made better arrangements. Did she hear the echo of that same divine chuckle I thought I'd heard?

As I held my son, I marveled at the grip of tiny fingers winding themselves around my heart, filling me with an overwhelming sense of responsibility and a fierce maternal love. Like Mary, I pondered the mysteries of life and incarnation. Why would God pour Himself into a helpless human infant who entered our world through the perils of birth in a cave where animals were stabled? I fought back tears as I sang quietly to my baby. *Silent night. . .holy night. . .All is calm. . .all is bright. . .*

The words made me pause. Things couldn't have been silent, holy, and calm that first Christmas night. Not as a mother and child labored and struggled and fought for life. And yet, somehow, having just gone through the process myself, I understood a deeper holy silence and a brighter calm than anything I had ever known. Somewhere beneath the obvious, beyond the visible, in the realm of the eternal, I could hear God orchestrating an oratorio that would forever celebrate His joy in birth. . .the birth of His Son. . . the birth of our sons and daughters. . .our rebirth as His children.

PATRICIA SOUDER

III

Heavenly Peace

Peace on Earth

Two thousand years ago
Angels sang Messiah's birth
And with it peace on earth.
Yet young and old of every race
In every place
Still shout and cry,
Still bleed and die,
Held hostage by hostility.

Two thousand years?
Were angels wrong to sing that song,
Since evil thrives and hate's still strong?
No! Young and old of every race
In every place
Take heart! Arise!
Emmanuel's cries
Shout peace for all eternity.

PATRICIA SOUDER

CHRISTMAS IN THE SOUTH

My wife and I had just retired from our ministry at a rescue mission in New York State, but we were eager to continue working in some way. Doors flew open for us in Bible conference work, and we found ourselves embarked on a new life in the South.

As the holidays approached, however, we began to feel uneasy. Most of our children were married, and they all had busy lives. We longed to be with them—but we were separated geographically now. We didn't want to be a burden or a nuisance to them. Even at this stage in our lives, we wanted to continue to be good role models. Talking often on the phone eased our pain. . .and we dove into God, asking Him to fill our lonely hearts.

God was faithful. Not only did our new church open their hearts to us, but our family drove hundreds of miles to visit us. New friends welcomed us into their homes. Children and grandchildren flooded us with their love.

Life's changes are often painful. As we grow older, our Christmases are not the same as they used to be. We have to let go of familiar traditions.

But through it all I hear God's voice: *Be still and know Me. Draw close to Me, and I will draw close to you.* (from Psalm 46:10, James 4:8). God's peace never fails.

TIM WYMBS

Remembering a Lifetime of Christmases

I close my eyes. . .and softly the strains of "Silent Night" flood my heart with Christmas memories. . . .

I see me as a child trudging through deep snow with Mom and Dad to the Christmas Eve Sunday school party. . . .

And then, another year, on a bitter cold night. . .I accompanied Gram to a Christmas cantata. What lingers in my memory is the way she held my hand so snuggly in hers.

Every year, my family exchanged Christmas presents, going round and round the circle, each person opening one gift at a time. . . . The memory of fresh pine scent, candlelight in the windows, and the Christmas village beneath the tree brings me a joy so sharp it almost hurts.

Years later, as an adult, I lived in Arizona, where star-filled nights and a nearby olive tree made me ponder Jesus' life in the desert. The wonder of starry skies and sturdy olive trees seemed to bring Him close, as though we shared something new in common.

Now, in my solemn twilight years, I find myself silently repeating the words of "Silent Night" to settle my soul. I have no family circle left to share gifts on Christmas morning. And yet I have learned the truth of an old saying: *For those who mourn, the Christ Child is born.* The peace of Christmas still sings.

Florence M. Hustedt

What can I give Him,
the baby Jesus,
on this holy night?
I have no gold, no myrrh, no frankincense.
My tithe on Sundays
doesn't count,
for it is rightfully yours, God.
I do not have a son,
no Isaac to offer you,
and if I did,
I doubt I'd be as strong in faith
As Abraham was.

I have only myself,
an old woman, a sinner,
wretched, lonely, at death's door.
Ah, but I can give my only treasure—
my heart, kept hidden deep inside me.
Here I am, Baby Jesus.
Please.
Receive me
as I am.

FLORENCE M. HUSTEDT

Peace comes from knowing we will never be rejected. He treasures each heart and fills us with the peace that passes all human understanding.

THE UNITY OF CHRISTMAS PEACE

My growing up years in New England were very different from my husband's childhood in northeastern Pennsylvania. Even our Christmas traditions were different.

Oh, we both had snow and jingle bells mingled with the familiar tunes of Christmas carols. But the December before our wedding, I noticed my fiancé lingering over toy trains every time we went shopping. He was especially fascinated with one that came complete with a miniature village. . . . As my fiancé hovered over this display, I waited patiently, wondering what this fascination with trains was all about. I knew young boys enjoyed playing with trains—but I was startled when my grown man said to me, "Don't you think we should buy a train if we're getting married? We'll need it next year."

Our budget was tight. . .and I couldn't help but wonder if he had lost his mind. Why would we possibly need a train?

In New England, of course, we put gifts under the Christmas tree. It never crossed my mind that my husband would expect a train under the tree. But that was the custom in northeastern Pennsylvania, a tradition my husband wanted to hand on to his children.

Our customs may have been different—but we shared the important Christmas items: shepherds watching their sheep, angels singing, and a Baby in the manger. Whatever our differences, that newborn King drew us together in His peace. . .just as He longs to unite us all.

MARY HERRON